COUNTRIES OF THE WORLD

Israel

Gareth Stevens Publishing
MILWAUKEE

About the Author: Frederick Fisher is a travel writer and novelist living in the United States. He and his wife have adventured extensively in Southeast Asia, and they spend six months on the Pacific Rim each year.

Written by
FREDERICK FISHER

Edited by
KEN CHANG

Designed by
HASNAH MOHD ESA

Picture research by
SUSAN JANE MANUEL

First published in North America in 2000 by
Gareth Stevens Publishing
1555 North RiverCenter Drive, Suite 201
Milwaukee, Wisconsin 53212 USA

For a free color catalog describing
Gareth Stevens' list of high-quality books
and multimedia programs, call
1-800-542-2595 (USA) or
1-800-461-9120 (CANADA).
Gareth Stevens Publishing's
Fax: (414) 225-0377.

© **TIMES EDITIONS PTE LTD 2000**
Originated and designed by
Times Editions Pte Ltd
Times Centre, 1 New Industrial Road
Singapore 536196
http://www.timesone.com.sg/te

Library of Congress Cataloging-in-Publication Data available upon request from publisher. Fax: (414) 225-0377 for the attention of the Publishing Records Department

ISBN 0-8368-2319-2

Printed in Malaysia

1 2 3 4 5 6 7 8 9 04 03 02 01 00

Contents

AN OVERVIEW OF ISRAEL

Although Israel declared its independence in 1948, its founding principle — the establishment of a Jewish state — is over 3,000 years old. A small, densely populated, Middle Eastern nation with an overwhelming range of geographical, ethnic, and religious diversity, the modern State of Israel has endured war, terrorism, and political controversy throughout its short history. Yet Israel remains an immensely powerful nation, driven by a resilient and prolific people who have excelled as artists, scientists, soldiers, industrialists, and statesmen. Today, Israel still serves as a heartfelt homeland for Jews around the world, and its various immigrant cultures have created a fascinating, international social world within its cities and settlements.

Opposite: Israel's capital, Jerusalem, is one of the oldest cities in the world.

Below: A group of Jewish teenagers sells citron and willow for Sukkot, a festival of thanksgiving.

THE FLAG OF ISRAEL

The design of the Israeli national flag was adopted in 1948. It dates back to 1891, when it was first used to represent Zionism, a cultural and political campaign whose goal was to create a Jewish state in Palestine (the ancient homeland of the Jews' early ancestors). The flag features two horizontal blue stripes and the Magen David (Shield of David) — a six-pointed star made from two triangles — on a white background. Jewish communities have used the Magen David as an official symbol since the 1600s. The flag's colors and stripes evoke the traditional design of a *tallith* (TAH-lis), or Jewish prayer shawl.

Geography

One of the smallest nations in the Middle East, the State of Israel has an area of 7,992 square miles (20,699 square kilometers) — excluding the disputed territories of East Jerusalem, the Gaza Strip, the Golan Heights, and the West Bank. The status of these territories, originally annexed by Israel after wars with its Arab neighbors, has still not been settled. The Israeli government and the Palestinian Council currently rule over separate areas within the Gaza Strip and the West Bank, while East Jerusalem and the Golan Heights remain solely under Israeli rule.

The Mediterranean Sea forms Israel's western boundary. The Gulf of Aqaba, an arm of the Red Sea that reaches out to southern Israel, offers a short, secondary coastline. Except for Jerusalem, which is about 30 miles (48 km) inland from the Mediterranean Sea, most of Israel's cities are concentrated on the western coastal plain. From west to east, the elevation steadily rises, topping out at the Hills of Judea and the mountains of Galilee, before dropping below sea level at various parts of the Jordan and Arava Valleys. Israel's immediate neighbors are Egypt (to the southwest), Jordan (to the east), Syria (to the northeast), and Lebanon (to the north).

Below: **The peaceful Sea of Galilee lies in northeastern Israel, where the government has set up a number of nature reserves.**

Deserts and Inland Seas

Stretching across Israel's southern frontier, the Negev is a vast, rocky, desert region that occupies more than a third of the country. Although traditionally a homeland for Arab nomads, the Negev has been reborn (with the help of modern irrigation methods) as a farming area for many Jewish settlers. Just north of the Negev lies the Judean Desert, a narrow strip of barren land separating Jerusalem and the salty Dead Sea, Israel's largest inland sea and the lowest body of water on Earth, at over 1,300 feet (396 meters) below sea level. The smaller Sea of Galilee, also known as Lake Kinneret or Lake Tiberias, lies southwest of the Golan Heights and supplies Israel's National Water Carrier, a system of canals and pipelines that provides water to a network of communities extending from the coastal plain all the way to the Negev.

The Jordan River

The chief waterway of Israel is the famous Jordan River, which descends from Mount Hermon in Syria, passes through the Sea of Galilee, and then empties into the Dead Sea. Meandering for over 223 miles (359 km), the Jordan is an important irrigation source for Israeli and Jordanian farmers, whose crops must survive in a very dry climate.

THE DEAD SEA

The aptly named Dead Sea is devoid of any life except for bacteria. While fishermen flock to the Sea of Galilee, the Dead Sea attracts a more unusual crowd of archaeologists, mud-bathers, and mining workers.

(A Closer Look, page 44)

Climatic Contrasts

Israel's climate is generally subtropical, although temperature and rainfall levels vary greatly with the distance from the Mediterranean Sea. Temperatures are coolest on the western coast, averaging a high of 84° Fahrenheit (29° Celsius) in August and a low of 48° F (9° C) in January. The Arava Valley is the hottest region of the country; in Eilat, summer temperatures can reach as high as 114° F (46° C).

The rainy season lasts from November through April. Annual rainfall ranges from 44 inches (112 centimeters) in northern Galilee to less than 1 inch (2.5 cm) in the Arava Valley. Tel Aviv-Yafo, on the Mediterranean coastal plain, receives 21 inches (53 cm) of annual rainfall.

Wildlife and Vegetation

More than 70 species of mammals, 80 species of reptiles, and 380 species of birds make their home in Israel. Common mammal predators include foxes, mongooses, hyenas, wolves, and wildcats. Plant- and insect-eating mammals include goats, ibexes, hares, porcupines, and hedgehogs.

Above: **During the hot summers, Israelis head west to cool off on the Mediterranean coast.**

Naturalists have identified over 2,800 plant species in Israel, ranging from pistachio trees in the Negev to honeysuckle in Galilee. Common flowers include red coral peonies, irises, Madonna lilies, tulips, and hyacinths. Forests and woodlands cover a small, but thriving, area of 469 square miles (1,215 square km). The Jewish National Fund (JNF), founded in 1901 to support Jewish settlers in the region that is now Israel, is largely responsible for the country's current level of forest growth. Between 1901 and 1948, the JNF sponsored a massive afforestation project which planted over 4.5 million trees.

National Parks

Israel has over 150 nature reserves, such as the Hai Bar Reserve (on the salt flats of the southern Negev), Mount Meron Nature Reserve (in Galilee), and Mount Carmel National Park (near Haifa). Overall, Israel's national parks attract some 2 million visitors every year. National wildlife preservation laws currently protect hundreds of endangered plants and animals, including oaks, palms, gazelles, leopards, and vultures.

Above: **The ibex, a type of mountain goat, is one of the many inhabitants of the Hai Bar Reserve.**

Below: **The Dead Sea appears behind a cactus garden in the city of En Gedi.**

History

Conquerors of the Holy Land

Canaan (also called the *Holy Land*) is the biblical name of Palestine, an area that stretches westward from the Jordan River to the Mediterranean Sea. In 1125 B.C., the Hebrews (descendants of the biblical Abraham, Isaac, and Jacob) conquered Canaan and became known as the Israelites. The Israelite monarchy reached its peak with King David, who, during the early tenth century B.C., united all twelve of the Israelite tribes, established Jerusalem as his capital, and reigned for nearly forty years. In 930 B.C., the Israelite kingdom split into Israel (northern Palestine) and Judah (southern Palestine).The Babylonians conquered Judah in 586 B.C. and forced many of the Israelites into exile in Babylon (in present-day Iraq). This exile marked the beginning of the Diaspora, or scattering of the Israelites (and their descendants) from their homeland. When the Israelites returned to Jerusalem in 538 B.C., they became known as Jews.

THE KINGS OF JUDAH

David and his son, Solomon, were the most successful kings of ancient Israel. Their legacy lives on in the Jewish faith, the Bible, and in the ruins of Jerusalem and the Negev. *(A Closer Look, page 58)*

Below: **The aqueducts of Caesarea were built by Herod the Great, who was appointed king of Judah by the Romans in 37 B.C.**

tonuus tei teuit: er afintauit ea in tarrar

Left: In 1095, European political and religious leaders launched the Crusades, a series of military campaigns to conquer Jerusalem (which had been taken over by Muslims in the seventh century) in the name of Christianity.

THE DOME OF THE ROCK

In A.D. 691, Muslim Arabs in Jerusalem completed the Dome of the Rock — one of the most magnificent buildings in the world. Today, the Dome of the Rock remains a sacred Islamic site and a strong reminder of Jerusalem's Muslim past.

(A Closer Look, page 46)

Over the next thousand years, Palestine passed through the hands of the Persians, Alexander the Great, the Romans, and the Byzantines. Jewish revolts against the Roman Empire in A.D. 66 led to the persecution, enslavement, and exile of hundreds of thousands of Jews. Nevertheless, determined Jewish communities, both within Palestine and abroad, held on tightly to their minority religion and culture. With the rise of Constantine the Great, the first Roman emperor to convert to Christianity, Palestine became a Christian stronghold in the fourth century A.D.

As the gateway between the East and the West, Palestine continued to attract new waves of foreign invaders. Muslim Arabs took over Palestine in A.D. 636, and Jerusalem soon became a new cultural and political base for Islam. In 1099, the crusading armies of Western Europe captured Jerusalem from the Muslims, but the crusaders' weak hold on the city was broken for good in the mid-thirteenth century. Muslim regimes controlled Palestine for another six hundred years — first the Mamluks, and then the Ottoman Turks, whose rule lasted from 1517 to 1917. As the Ottoman Empire opened up to foreign settlements in the late 1800s, the Jewish diaspora planned a return to the Holy Land.

Below: Alexander the Great of Macedonia conquered Palestine in 333 B.C., a year before he successfully invaded Egypt.

Eretz Yisra'el

Although most Jews of the Diaspora had completely integrated themselves into Western culture, they continued to face anti-Semitic persecution. By the late nineteenth century, Zionism — a nationalist movement among Jews to return to *Eretz Yisra'el*, or the Land of Israel — was gaining momentum in Europe. In 1897, Austrian journalist Theodor Herzl (1860–1904) organized the first Zionist Congress in Basel, Switzerland and established Zionism as an international political campaign. Almost 2,500 years after their Babylonian exile and 1,800 years after they were conquered by the Romans, the Jews readied themselves for a mass return to their home in Palestine.

Zionism still faced many obstacles, however, since it was a small movement with a thinly spread support base. Additionally, as outsiders based in Europe and North America, the Zionists were not well-received by Middle Eastern leaders. The Ottoman government rejected Herzl's proposal to create an independent Jewish settlement in Palestine, and Jewish immigrants in Palestine had to be financially supported by the diaspora. By 1914, Jewish settlers in Palestine numbered only about 90,000.

Above: Theodor Herzl was the political spark behind the Zionist movement. In February 1896, he published *The Jewish State,* which argued that Jews must unite behind a political body in order to be heard by the world.

The Balfour Declaration

After World War I broke out in 1914, Zionist leaders won the backing of the British government, which supported the Zionist cause and also hoped to gain worldwide Jewish support for its war effort against Germany. On November 2, 1917, British foreign secretary Arthur J. Balfour issued a letter to London-based Zionist leaders that pledged British support for the establishment of a Jewish state in Palestine. The Balfour Declaration is considered an important document of modern Jewish history. In 1922, the League of Nations (now the United Nations) granted Great Britain a mandate to govern Palestine. By 1933, the Jewish population of Palestine had grown to 238,000.

INDEPENDENCE DAY

Israel's annual Independence Day is not just a national holiday but a momentous occasion celebrated by Jews and non-Jews all over the world. In 1998, the State of Israel celebrated its fiftieth birthday.
(*A Closer Look*, page 50)

From the Holocaust to Independence

With the rise of Adolf Hitler in Germany during the 1930s, 165,000 European Jews migrated to British-controlled Palestine. The Jews who remained in Europe faced a Nazi campaign of genocide. During the Holocaust of World War II, more than six million Jews were exterminated in concentration camps.

After the war ended in 1945, Zionist leaders worked feverishly to facilitate the immigration of surviving European Jews to Palestine. On May 14, 1948, David Ben-Gurion, the chairman of the Zionist Executive, proclaimed the establishment of the Jewish state in Palestine to be called *Medinat Yisra'el* (the State of Israel).

Above: **Between 1940 and 1945, more than one million Jews died in the Nazi extermination camp in Auschwitz, Poland. Prisoners were brought into the camp on freight trains and marked with badges shaped in the form of the Magen David.**

Left: **French president Jacques Chirac and PLO chairman Yasir Arafat greet a member of the Jewish community in the West Bank. European and American leaders play an important part in the Arab-Israeli peace process.**

The Struggle for Peace

The Arabs of the Middle East refused to accept the State of Israel. On May 15, 1948, the armies of Egypt, Transjordan (now Jordan), Syria, Lebanon, and Iraq joined Palestinian Arabs in a war against Israel. Although greatly outnumbered, the Israel Defense Forces (IDF) successfully stood their ground against the Arab invaders.

In 1956, war broke out again after Egypt blockaded Israeli shipping through the Gulf of Aqaba and signed a military alliance with Syria and Jordan. In response, the IDF seized the Gaza Strip and the Sinai Peninsula (withdrawing in 1957). The Six-Day War erupted in 1967, after Egyptian, Jordanian, and Syrian troops amassed near Israel's western, eastern, and northern borders, respectively; Israel struck first and won control of the Gaza Strip, the Sinai Peninsula, East Jerusalem, the West Bank, and the Golan Heights. In the Yom Kippur War of 1973, Egypt and Syria jointly attacked Israel but were eventually repelled by the IDF.

In 1978, Israeli prime minister Menachem Begin and Egyptian president Anwar Sadat signed the Camp David Accords, which established peaceful relations between their two countries. New conflicts, however, arose between Israel and the Palestine Liberation Organization (PLO), which used terrorist attacks in its efforts to create a Palestinian state. Today, the Israelis are in the process of granting self-rule to Palestinians in the West Bank and Gaza Strip.

THE ENTEBBE RESCUE

In 1976, Palestinian terrorists hijacked an airliner en route from Israel to France and forced it to land in Entebbe, Uganda. Israeli commandos carried out a daring rescue mission that saved 103 lives.
(A Closer Look, page 48)

PALESTINIANS

While Jews around the world celebrated the founding of Israel in 1948, more than one million native Palestinian Arabs (whose ancestors had lived in Palestine for several hundreds of years) were suddenly denied self-rule. The Palestinian struggle for independence continues today.
(A Closer Look, page 64)

David Ben-Gurion (1886–1973)

Regarded as the father of modern Israel, David Ben-Gurion dedicated his life to the Zionist cause. In 1906, a young David Gruen left his home in Poland for Palestine, where he renamed himself Ben-Gurion ("Son of the Lion" in Hebrew) and worked as a farmer alongside fellow Zionist pioneers. On May 14, 1948, he delivered Israel's declaration of independence to the Israeli people. As the nation's first prime minister (serving from 1948 to 1953 and again from 1955 to 1963), Ben-Gurion welded together a strong nation that ably faced the challenges of desert settlement, mass immigration, and Arab threats.

David Ben-Gurion

Golda Meir (1898–1978)

One of the founders of the State of Israel, Golda Meir served as a member of parliament, cabinet minister, and diplomat before becoming prime minister in 1969. Born Goldie Mabovich in Kiev, Ukraine, she grew up in the United States (where she married Morris Myerson) before immigrating to Palestine in 1921. A passionate Zionist leader, she was appointed minister of labor in 1949. In 1956, Goldie Myerson adopted the Hebrew name Golda Meir and took the post of foreign minister, which she held for ten years. In 1969, Meir became the first and (so far) only woman prime minister of Israel. She remained in power until the Yom Kippur War, which ultimately resulted in her resignation in 1974.

Golda Meir

Yitzhak Rabin (1922–1995)

Yitzhak Rabin succeeded Golda Meir as Israel's prime minister in 1974 and later served a second term beginning in 1992. A decorated army veteran, Rabin first entered politics in 1973. As a statesman, he was known for trying to secure a lasting peace between Israel and its Palestinian and Arab neighbors. In 1993, Rabin's government signed the Israel-PLO accords, which recognized the PLO and the Palestinians' need for autonomy. A year later, Rabin and Jordan's King Hussein signed a joint peace treaty. Rabin, Israeli foreign minister Shimon Peres, and PLO chairman Yasir Arafat received the Nobel Prize for Peace in 1994. Sadly, Prime Minister Rabin was assassinated by a Jewish extremist on November 4, 1995.

Yitzhak Rabin

Government and the Economy

Political Structure

Israel is a parliamentary republic whose government consists of legislative, executive, and judicial branches. The Knesset, or legislative body, is a unicameral parliament made up of 120 members. Elected every four years, Knesset members are responsible for writing and debating laws and keeping executive power in check. The Knesset also operates through fourteen standing committees that deal with issues such as defense, immigration, social welfare, and the status of women.

Elected by the Knesset, the president serves as the nation's head of state and carries out mostly ceremonial duties. Israel's executive power rests in the prime minister (who is elected by

Below: **The Knesset is the lawmaking body of the government. The State of Israel has no official constitution; previous laws passed by the Knesset have set up the framework for the current political structure.**

popular vote every four years) and the cabinet of ministers (who are appointed by the prime minister but must be approved by the Knesset). The prime minister is allowed to name between eight and eighteen cabinet ministers, at least half of whom must be Knesset members. The executive branch is in charge of administering internal and foreign affairs.

Israel's judiciary system is independent from the legislative and executive branches. As the highest court of appeal, the Supreme Court can change rulings made by lower district and magistrate courts.

Elections

Israeli citizens are entitled to vote once they reach the age of eighteen. No single political party has ever achieved a majority in the Knesset. Today, two major political blocs dominate Israeli politics: the Labor Party, a social democratic party founded in 1968, and the Likud party, a conservative group established in 1973. Several other parties (representing ethnic, religious, or special interest groups) play significant roles in the Knesset. Voters cast two ballots: one for a prime minister candidate, and the other for a parliamentary party. Each party is then assigned a percentage of the seats in the Knesset based on the vote.

Above: **Labor Party candidate Ehud Barak** *(left)* **won the 1999 election for prime minister. He is a former Chief of the General Staff of the Israel Defense Forces and one of Israel's most decorated soldiers. Barak's opponent was incumbent and Likud party leader Benjamin Netanyahu** *(right).* **A former ambassador to the United Nations, Netanyahu became the first Israeli prime minister to be elected by popular vote in 1996.**

Economic Challenges

Israel faces costly economic challenges. Over 10 percent of Israel's gross domestic product (GDP) is spent on national defense — training, arming, and maintaining the elite IDF. Another economic challenge is handling the continuing inflow of immigrants, who require housing, health and social services, and, if they are unskilled, education. The Israeli government also has very high standards for building a modern infrastructure and providing the best public services possible for its people.

The economy has grown rapidly to meet these challenges, but the Israeli government still faces ballooning debts. In 1996, Israel's national deficit exceeded U.S. $20 billion, mostly because of its trade imbalance (Israel imports more goods than it exports). The government relies on foreign aid and loans to help bear these costs.

Industry, Agriculture, and Trade

Israel's leading industries include telecommunications, chemicals, electronics, and diamond cutting and polishing. Israel produces roughly 80 percent of the world's output of small polished gems. High-tech products (such as pharmaceuticals and computers) make up 80 percent of Israel's industrial exports.

Above: **Yafo, the seaport of Tel Aviv-Yafo, is one of Israel's major trading ports. Further north, Tel Aviv is the heart of Israeli industry and scientific research.**

ISRAEL DEFENSE FORCES (IDF)

Despite usually being outnumbered in battle, the Israel Defense Forces have a reputation for victory. Today, the IDF is among the elite national armed forces organizations in the world. Military service is required for most Israelis, both men and women.
(A Closer Look, page 52)

Modern science paved the way for Israel's agricultural sector, which depends on advanced irrigation technology. Major agricultural products include citrus fruits, vegetables, poultry, and dairy products. Israeli farming settlements can be split up into two main types: the kibbutz, or collective settlement, in which people share equally in the work and the profits; and the *moshav* (moh-SHAHV), or cooperative settlement, in which individual farms are worked separately but the produce is pooled together.

Israel's main imports are raw materials, such as fossil fuels and rough diamonds. Major exports include finished diamonds, electronics, textiles, and fertilizers. The United States, Belgium, Germany, and Great Britain are Israel's main trading partners.

Histadrut

Founded in 1920, the Histadrut, or New General Federation of Labor, is Israel's largest trade union, representing all economic sectors. Histadrut members receive benefits such as health insurance, welfare and legal services, and vocational training.

THE KIBBUTZ

The kibbutz, a uniquely Israeli social, cultural, and economic unit, represents the traditional model of national agriculture. Today, over 120,000 *kibbutzniks* (key-BOOTS-niks), or kibbutz settlers, live on some 270 kibbutzim.
(A Closer Look, page 56)

Below: **Palestinians harvest chilies on a farm in the Gaza Strip.**

People and Lifestyle

Israel's population has grown rapidly due to a steady influx of Jewish immigrants from all over the world. The immigration of Russian Jews to Palestine dates back to the late 1800s. Waves of European Jews arrived in the 1930s and late 1940s, while a number of North African Jews arrived in the 1950s. Today, 81 percent of Israel's 5.8 million people are Jews, more than half of whom are *sabras* (ZAH-braz), or Israeli-born Jews; the remaining immigrant Israeli Jews come from over 70 countries around the world.

The 1.1 million non-Jews in Israel are collectively defined as the Arab citizens of Israel, although a handful of them are not ethnically Arab but rather only Arabic-speaking. This minority group includes Muslims, Christians, Druze, and Circassians.

Left: **Hasidic Jews wear very traditional, black clothing, and the men's hairstyles feature curly side-locks. Hasidism is an ultraorthodox form of Judaism that stresses prayer mysticism and certain rules governing marriage, diet, birth, and death.**

Ethno-Religious Groups

Because of their immigrant backgrounds, Israeli Jews represent a
variety of European, African, Asian, and American ethnic groups.
The two main cultural groups within the Jewish population are
the Ashkenazim, whose ancestors originated in Central and
Eastern Europe, and the Sephardim, whose ancestors originated
in Spain, North Africa, and the Middle East. The two groups
differ in worship rituals and some ethnic traditions. More than
80 percent of the world's Jews are Ashkenazim.

Almost all of the non-Jewish Israeli population is ethnically
Arab. Muslim Arabs, numbering about 843,000, and Christian
Arabs, numbering 180,000, are the two largest groups. The
Bedouin Arabs make up 8 percent of the Muslim Arab
population. They were formerly nomadic shepherds who
inhabited Galilee and the Negev, but, today, they are gradually
entering Israel's labor force. Generally, Muslim Arabs live in
rural settlements, while Christian Arabs prefer a more urban
lifestyle. The Druze, numbering 96,000, are an Arabic-speaking
people who practice a secret religion that has survived for almost
a thousand years. Smaller minority groups include the
Circassians (who are Muslims but not Arabs) and the Samaritans
(who are neither Muslims nor Arabs).

**MINORITY
CULTURES**

Israel's immigrant
society boasts many
minority groups,
such as Arabs, Druze,
Ethiopians, Bedouins,
and Circassians.

(A Closer Look, page 60)

Family Life

The majority of Israeli Jews are non-Orthodox Jews, whose religious practices are less observant (or more modern) than those of Orthodox Jews, who strictly follow the traditional ways of Judaism. Religion has a big impact on Israeli family life — it affects parenting, education, and social interaction. For instance, Orthodox families tend to be large, with seven to twelve children, while non-Orthodox families tend to have only two to three children. Orthodox parents also require strict religious observance and schooling, and may even limit their children's interaction with non-Orthodox Jews. In contrast, less observant Jews are more open to the social diversity offered by Israel's immigrant culture. Many non-Orthodox Jews have very Western-oriented, nuclear-family lifestyles.

Non-Jewish families live very freely and independently in Israel, despite their minority status in a Jewish state. Muslim, Christian, and Druze families are often supported by small and protective ethnic or religious communities.

MITZVAHS

A *mitzvah* (MITTS-vah) is a biblical commandment or guideline upon which Jews base their moral conduct. One important mitzvah is to "be fruitful and multiply." Orthodox Jews tend to take this advice more seriously than non-Orthodox Jews, which explains why an Orthodox family often has several more children than a non-Orthodox family. In total, there are 613 mitzvahs.

Rural and Urban Communities

More than 90 percent of Israelis live in urban areas. Israel's major cities are Jerusalem (the national capital and spiritual center), Tel Aviv-Yafo (the industrial center), and Haifa (the trading and commerce center). Together, these three cities account for 25 percent of Israel's population. Jews and Arabs often live in separate neighborhoods, giving each city a dual character.

The classic Israeli rural community is the kibbutz, a self-contained group of families that functions as one collective unit. Decisions are made democratically, and members are assigned work in different branches of the kibbutz economy. Today, kibbutzim are outnumbered by moshavim, which allow individual families more independence than their kibbutznik counterparts. Arabs and Druze make up one-sixth of Israel's rural population, operating small farms and businesses.

JERUSALEM

Jerusalem is much more than Israel's capital city; for Jews, Christians, and Muslims alike, it is a holy city, home to many sacred sites and shrines. For almost 5,000 years, Jerusalem has served as a crossroads for religion, arts, commerce, language, and politics.
(A Closer Look, page 54)

Left: A street musician cradles his violin on a Jerusalem sidewalk.

Education

Israel's history of educating its people actually predates the establishment of the country. The Technion-Israel Institute of Technology in Haifa was founded in 1924, and the Hebrew University of Jerusalem was founded in 1925 — not long after the first kibbutzim were set up in Palestine by Russian and European Jews.

After the State of Israel declared independence in 1948, one of the first laws passed by the new government was the Compulsory Education Law of 1949. Under this law, the state provides free and compulsory elementary education for all children between the ages of five and fourteen years old; amendments to the law have extended the upper age limit to eighteen years old. The biggest challenge facing the Israeli education system is maintaining high academic standards while student enrollment expands with continuing immigration. Another important goal is providing an equal and appropriate education for all students, while respecting differences in cultural background.

Above: **At the Yonatan Elementary School in Netanya, students listen attentively to a presentation given by one of their classmates.**

Israeli children begin school at age five, with a year of kindergarten, followed by six years of primary school. At age twelve, students attend three years of junior high school, followed by another three years of high school. Two parallel state-school systems — one for Jews, with classes taught in Hebrew, and another for Arabs and Druze, with classes taught in Arabic — educate Israeli students separately. High-school students can choose to prepare for university studies, agricultural schools, trade schools, religious academies (yeshivas), or military schools. Over 30 percent of Israeli students continue their education after graduating from high school. Besides the Technion and the Hebrew University of Jerusalem, Israel's major universities include the Weizmann Institute of Science in Rehovet, Bar-Ilan University in Ramat Gan, and Tel Aviv University. The Ministry of Education also provides adult education classes for new immigrants.

TALMUDIC STUDIES

At yeshivas, or Jewish religious schools, students study the Bible, the Talmud (a collection of legal writings by Jewish scholars), and other religious literature.
(A Closer Look, page 68)

Left: A student rally gathers momentum in the streets of Jerusalem. Israeli high-school and university students are among the most intelligent and politically active in the world.

Religion in the Jewish State

Israel's main religions are Judaism, Islam, Christianity, Druze, and Bahaism. While Jewish culture is apparent in daily Israeli life, minority religions form a crucial part of Israel's national character.

Judaism is a monotheistic religion that first appeared almost 3,500 years ago. Jews recognize Abraham (c. 2000 B.C.) as the founder of Judaism, although the Mishna, the first collection of Jewish laws, did not exist in written form until 200 A.D. Many Jewish traditions and practices are based on the Torah (the first five books of the Bible, also known as the Pentateuch) and the Talmud (a legal book of interpretations of the Mishna produced by Jewish scholars around A.D. 500). Besides placing their faith in one divine God, Jews also believe that their ancestors, the Hebrews, were specifically chosen and blessed by God, and that this relationship continues with the current Jewish community.

The three main branches of Judaism are Orthodox, Reform, and Conservative. Developed in late 1700s, Reform Judaism brought social reforms to Orthodox Judaism, whose followers maintain strict rules regarding worship, diet, and lifestyle. Reform Jews also argued for the separation of one's religious identity from one's national identity. Conservative Judaism lies between the

Above: **Hasidic Jews are a small but united Orthodox minority in Israel. Although Israel exists as a Jewish state, it has no official religion and guarantees freedom of religion to its people.**

THE WESTERN WALL

The Western Wall, in East Jerusalem, is a holy Jewish site that is over two thousand years old.

(A Closer Look, page 70)

extremes of Reform and Orthodox. In both Reform and Conservative communities, the genders are more integrated than in the segregated, male-dominated Orthodox community. In Reform or Conservative Judaism, a woman may be ordained as a rabbi (the chief religious official of a synagogue).

The Muslim community of Israel is made up of Arabs and Circassians. Jerusalem had been under Muslim control for some 1,300 years before Israelis claimed the city as their capital in 1948, and strong Islamic influences remain today. Christian Arab communities are mainly Greek Catholic, Greek Orthodox, or Roman Catholic. Galilee, where Jesus Christ began his teachings, and Jerusalem, where he was crucified, are among the most holy places in the Christian world. The Druze are monotheists who keep their religion a secret from outsiders; they do not allow intermarriage or conversion to other religions. The Baha'i faith, founded in 1844 in Iran, is a universal religion whose spiritual center is in Acre, in northeastern Israel. Baha'is believe that all the world's religions teach the same message.

The gleaming Dome of the Rock *(above)* is a holy Muslim shrine; the Church of the Holy Sepulcher *(below)* stands on the sacred site of Christ's crucifixion. Both monuments are located in Jerusalem.

Language and Literature

Israel is a multilingual country, with Hebrew as its official
and most commonly used language, and Arabic as its second
language. Many Israelis also speak English, Yiddish, Russian,
or any European language consistent with their heritage.

Originally, Jews only used Hebrew as their language of study
and prayer, but, today, Hebrew is a flourishing, living language.
Educational reform made it necessary to teach a common
language to Israel's new immigrants. The revival of Hebrew

Left: **An Israeli Arab
casually reads a
newspaper in the
Muslim Quarter of
Old Jerusalem.**

Left: Druze men buy books from a vendor in Galilee.

was largely the work of Eliezer Ben-Yehuda (1858–1922), who pioneered the development of a modern and dynamic language for the Israeli people. In 1890, Ben-Yehuda cofounded the Hebrew Language Committee, which updated the Hebrew vocabulary and promoted the use of Hebrew in schools and books. In 1959, scholars completed a seventeen-volume dictionary of ancient and modern Hebrew, which had been unfinished at the time of Ben-Yehuda's death.

Below: Born in Jerusalem in 1936, A. B. Yehoshua is a distinguished writer of novels, essays, and plays. In 1995, he received the Israel Prize for Literature.

Literature

The Zionist movement of the late 1800s brought attention to a number of Hebrew literary figures from Eastern Europe, such as novelist Shmuel Yosef Agnon (1888–1970), who was a co-recipient of the Nobel Prize for Literature in 1966, and Haim Nahman Bailik (1873–1934), who is regarded as Israel's national poet. The "war of independence generation," or native-born Israeli writers who published in the 1940s and 1950s, often expressed their strong commitment to a new society and state. Modern Israeli prose writers include A. B. Yehoshua, Amos Oz, Yoram Kaniuk, and Yaakov Shabtai.

Arts

Fine Arts

In 1906, Bulgarian-born sculptor Boris Schatz founded the Bezalel Academy of Arts and Crafts in Jerusalem. Bezalel's artistic goal was to create an "original Jewish art" that combined European and Middle Eastern influences. By the mid-1920s, newer immigrant artists were challenging Bezalel's nationalistic style in their search for a new cultural identity. Many leading artists of this period gravitated toward the young city of Tel Aviv (established in 1909), which still remains the center of Israel's dynamic art scene. Israeli art is not just an urban phenomenon; some of the nation's most inventive painters and sculptors are rural kibbutzniks.

Left: **A sculpture depicting the tragedy of the Nazi concentration camps stands at the Yad Vashem Museum in Jerusalem. The haunting scars left by World War II on the Jewish community have influenced countless visual artists, writers, and musicians.**

Classical Music

Classical music has always played an important role in Jewish cultural life. The Israel Philharmonic Orchestra (originally the Palestine Philharmonic Orchestra) collaborates with a number of world-famous conductors and soloists each year. Founded by renowned Polish-born violinist Bronislaw Huberman, the orchestra performed its first concert in 1936, under the direction of Italian virtuoso conductor Arturo Toscanini. Today, the Israel Philharmonic Orchestra represents the cornerstone of the national music scene and an unparalleled artistic triumph. Other classical orchestras and choral groups include the Jerusalem Symphony Orchestra (the first Israeli orchestra to broadcast its concerts on radio), the Israel Chamber Orchestra, the Haifa Symphony Orchestra, and the Tel Aviv Choir. Israel's national opera company, the New Israeli Opera, is based in Tel Aviv and attracts a dedicated following.

Israel hosts a number of classical music events, ranging from the Chamber Music Festival at Kibbutz Kfar Blum to the international Arthur Rubinstein Piano Competition. Among Israel's elite crop of classical virtuosos are violinist Itzhak Perlman, pianist-conductor Daniel Barenboim, and violinist-violist-conductor Pinchas Zukerman. Young Israelis interested in music studies can choose from over two hundred conservatories and hundreds of private teachers.

OPERA

Opera is one of the most exciting art forms in Israel. The New Israeli Opera combines the talents of both local and foreign opera artists.
(*A Closer Look, page 62*)

Left: **A trombonist in a klezmer band plays at a Jewish folk music festival.**

Folk Music

A strong tradition of folk music also thrives in Israel. The roots of Jewish religious and popular music date to the ancient Israelite kingdom — almost three thousand years ago. Today, the range of traditional Jewish songs has widened considerably as a result of far-flung Jewish communities assimilating various other cultures into their music. Klezmer, which stems from Eastern European Jewish culture, is one of the most popular forms of traditional folk music in Israel and in Jewish communities around the world.

Above: **Jewish folk dancers are among the liveliest entertainers in Israel.**

Theater and Dance

Habimah, Israel's national theater, was founded in Moscow in 1917 and moved to Tel Aviv in 1931. Originally established as a creative outlet for Zionist playwrights and dramatists, Habimah now stages both traditional and contemporary Hebrew works, as well as translated classics from American and European theater.

Folk dancing is an age-old Jewish art form that has strong Eastern European, Arabic, and North African influences. Since 1988, the town of Karmiel in central Galilee has hosted a three-day international folk dance festival that features performances by dance troupes from Israel and around the world. Modern dance and classical ballet are also popular in Israel.

Cinema

Since its beginnings in the 1950s, Israeli film has covered a wide range of thematic approaches, from documenting the Holocaust experience to portraying the alienation of modern-day Israelis. Today, most Israeli filmmakers choose to examine their nation's complex cultural identity by depicting the bare reality of Israeli life.

The Israel Film Center, a division of the Ministry of Trade and Industry, helps promote Israeli films overseas and offers funding for local film production. Israeli cinema is also supported by the Spielberg Film Archive (at the Hebrew University of Jerusalem) and the Jerusalem Cinemathéque (a film archive, research library, and theater hall).

Museums

Attracting over 10 million visitors every year, Israel's 120 museums feature exhibits on contemporary art, religious art, ethnic arts, history, archaeology, and architecture. The Tel Aviv Museum of Art houses one of the most comprehensive art collections in Israel, featuring modern and classical works by both local and foreign artists. The Israel Museum, founded in 1965 in Jerusalem, exhibits traditional Jewish artwork, modern paintings and sculptures, and an impressive display of historical artifacts (including the famous Dead Sea Scrolls, which contain the earliest biblical scriptures ever written). The Yad Vashem Museum, also in Jerusalem, is dedicated to the memory of the six million Jews who perished in the Holocaust.

ZIPPORI

The archaeological site of Zippori is filled with beautiful art and architecture. This city in Galilee used to be the ancient Jewish cultural capital of Palestine until it fell into ruin.
(A Closer Look, page 72)

Below: **The Tel Aviv Museum of Art was founded in 1926. In addition to its main galleries, the museum features a sculpture garden, a children's wing, and a performing arts theater.**

33

Leisure and Festivals

In Search of Fun

Israeli Jews are a hard-working people, taking only one day off — the *Shabbat* (shah-BAHT), or Sabbath — each week. In the cities, Israelis enjoy themselves by shopping, nightclubbing, playing sports, catching a movie, attending a concert, or chatting with friends at a café or restaurant. In Jerusalem, Ben Yehuda street offers a hip and stylish hangout for young Israelis, with its many boutiques, cafés, and street performers. Tel Aviv, Israel's artistic center, is dotted with fascinating museums and galleries. People looking to venture out of the city often head to the beach (either the Mediterranean coast or the resort town of Eilat by the Gulf of Aqaba). Another popular getaway is the Sea of Galilee, which is famous for its historical religious sites and its soothing hot springs. Generally, Israelis like to spend time outdoors, even for simple pleasures like a game of chess or backgammon.

In rural Israel, leisure time is more oriented toward the family and local community. Kibbutznik children spend their free time with their family and also with a designated peer group.

Below: **A young group of friends enjoys the cozy atmosphere of a Jerusalem café.**

Left: **Many Israelis enjoy playing backgammon outdoors in city parks.**

Reading to Relax

Israelis read more books per capita than any other people in the world. Israel has over a thousand public and private libraries, where avid readers can comfortably sit back with a book or magazine. Bookstores, book fairs, and literature readings are prized by both intellectuals and casual readers.

Israel's nation of readers has created an active market for publishers of books, newspapers, and magazines. To accommodate the various ethnic backgrounds of Israeli readers, books and periodicals are usually published in many languages, including Hebrew, English, Yiddish, German, Arabic, Russian, and French.

Sports

Soccer, basketball, swimming, tennis, volleyball, track and field, gymnastics, judo, and fencing are among the most popular sports in Israel. Indoor ice-skating rinks offer a cooler alternative to outdoor sports in the desert heat. Water sportsmen can try sailing, snorkeling, deep-sea diving, and windsurfing. Recently, indoor rock climbing has become a trendy sport among Israeli youths. Soccer and basketball are Israel's most popular spectator sports. Every year, thousands of Israelis participate in mass sporting events, such as the Jerusalem March, the swim across the Sea of Galilee, and various marathons.

Above: **Windsurfers enjoy the waves off the coast of Tel Aviv-Yafo.**

The Sports Authority of the Ministry of Education maintains a demanding physical education system in schools and also organizes local, regional, and national sports leagues. Athletic facilities are funded by both the Ministry of Education and private sports clubs. Israel's four major sports organizations are Maccabi, Betar, Hapoel, and Elizur. The Maccabi Tel Aviv basketball team won the European Cup championship in 1977 and again in 1981.

In basketball, soccer, and volleyball, Israel's national teams play in European leagues; for all other competitive sports, Israel belongs to the Asian Games Federation.

The Maccabiah Games

The international Maccabiah Games, also known as the Jewish Olympics, were first hosted in Palestine in 1932. Although competition was suspended after 1935 (due to the Nazi movement in Germany), the Maccabiah Games resumed in 1950. Today, the games attract over 3,600 Jewish athletes from thirty-five countries. Events include track and field, swimming, boxing, soccer, karate, and volleyball.

Israeli Olympians

Israel has competed at the Olympic Games since 1952. During the 1972 Olympic Games in Munich, Germany, tragedy struck as Palestinian terrorists murdered eleven Israeli athletes in an unsuccessful attempt to win the release of two hundred Arab terrorists imprisoned in Israel. In the 1992 Olympic Games in Barcelona, Israel won its first Olympic medals, in judo.

Left: **Two Israeli karate students spar in a martial arts youth club.**

Religious Holidays and Festivals

The Shabbat is the seventh day of the week and the designated day of rest. Public transportation stops, shops are closed, and the streets become empty. Orthodox Jews spend the Sabbath in prayer at home or in a *shul* (SHOOL), or synagogue. Non-Orthodox Jews are more likely to attend a Friday-night synagogue service and spend the Sabbath as a weekend holiday.

Rosh Hashanah, the Jewish New Year, begins on the first day of *Tishri* (TISH-ree), the first month of the Jewish calendar (usually occurring in September or October on the Gregorian calendar). Celebrations continue until the second day of Tishri. Yom Kippur, the holiest Jewish holiday, falls on the tenth day of Tishri. Jews pray for forgiveness for their sins and fast for a full day, from sunset on the eve of Yom Kippur to sunset on the next day. Sukkot (the Feast of Tabernacles), occurs five days after Yom Kippur and celebrates both the harvest and the Exodus of the Hebrews from Egypt.

Hanukkah begins on the twenty-fifth day of *Kislev* (KEYS-lev), the third month of the Jewish calendar. This celebration commemorates the Jews' rededication of the Second Temple of Jerusalem in A.D. 165, after it had been desecrated by the Romans. Jews observe Hanukkah for eight days, during which they pray, play games, and exchange gifts with their families.

Above: Jews assemble at the Western Wall for a *bar mitzvah* (bar MITTS-vah) ceremony. A bar mitzvah celebrates the initiation of a boy into the adult Jewish community at the age of thirteen. For girls, this coming-of-age ceremony is known as a *bat mitzvah* (baht MITTS-vah).

PASSOVER

Jews celebrate the liberation of their Hebrew ancestors from slavery on Passover, one of the most festive Jewish holidays of the year.

(*A Closer Look, page 66*)

Purim is a joyous, springtime holiday when Jews remember how their ancestors were saved from Haman, a Persian whose plan to eradicate the Jews backfired and cost him his own life. Pesach, or Passover, begins on the fourteenth day of *Nisan* (NEE-san), the seventh Jewish month, and lasts seven days. Passover celebrates one of the most important events in Jewish history, the Exodus, which happened over three thousand years ago.

Important Muslim holidays include Ramadan (a holy month of fasting), Eid al-Fitr (Feast of the Breaking of the Fast), and Eid al-Adha (Feast of the Sacrifice). Major Christian holidays are Christmas, Good Friday, and Easter.

Secular Holidays

Israel's secular holidays include Independence Day, Memorial Day (which remembers the soldiers who died defending Israel), and Holocaust Memorial Day (which remembers the Jews lost in the Holocaust of World War II).

Above: Clowns and carnivals are part of the fun festivities on Purim.

Below: The lighting of the menorah is an old Hanukkah tradition.

Food

Immigrant Cuisines

Israeli cuisine is a mixture of traditional Jewish, Eastern European, Middle Eastern, and North African foods. Jewish favorites include gefilte fish, or fish balls made from finely minced carp, pike, or pickerel; *kishkes* (KISH-keys), or roasted meat casings filled with flour, chicken fat, and onions; and *knaidlach* (NAYD-lock), or boiled dumplings made from eggs and *matzo* (MAHT-suh) meal. Crusty, doughnut-shaped bagels and soft, braided *challah* (KHAH-lah) are two kinds of Jewish bread that are found all over the world.

Immigrants from Russia, Poland, and Hungary brought their native cravings for rich and heavy foods, such as *cholent* (KHO-lent), which is a meat-and-potato stew, and *knishes* (KNISH-es), which are baked turnovers containing a potato filling. Other classic Eastern European dishes include *borscht* (BOHR-shta), a soup containing beets, meat, and vegetables,

Below: **A woman buys bagels at a Jewish market in Jerusalem.**

Left: **In coastal Israel, fresh fish is part of everyday cuisine.**

served either hot or cold, sometimes with sour cream; *latkes* (LAHT-keys), or fried potato pancakes; the ravioli-like *pirozhki* (pi-ROSH-key), stuffed with chopped meat or vegetables; and *kasha* (KAH-shah), a kind of buckwheat.

Middle Eastern Arabs have introduced more spicy dishes, such as falafel, a deep-fried ball of mashed chickpeas, garlic, and onions that is often served in pita bread. Shashliks are made from marinated cubes of meat that are skewered and roasted. North African immigrants introduced their desert-style cuisine of olives, dates, dried foods, and flat bread.

Restrictions on Eating

The Jewish dietary laws, or *kashrut* (kahsh-ROOT), do not allow certain foods and food preparations. For example, pork and shellfish are not eaten because they are prohibited by the Torah. Additionally, dairy products are never served with or cooked with meat. Kosher, or proper, foods must be prepared and served using two sets of dishes and two sets of cooking utensils — one used for preparing milk-based foods and the other for meat preparations. Animals must also be slaughtered in a certain way in order for their meat to be considered kosher.

Muslims also have their own set of dietary laws, which prohibit alcoholic beverages and certain meats. Muslim butchers must slaughter animals according to Islamic ritual.

Below: **A Druze woman serves up a plate of fresh bread.**

A CLOSER LOOK AT ISRAEL

Israel is a young country, a fact evident in its language, art, government, and people, whose average age is twenty-seven. Much of Israeli culture is vibrant, energetic, and new. Yet, another side of Israel is extremely old. Jewish history began over three thousand years ago, with the Israelite kingdom. Jerusalem and the Dead Sea lie at one of the oldest and most traveled crossroads in the world, where European, African, Middle Eastern, and Asian cultures clashed and connected. Today, Israeli society is both old and modern, just like it is both conservative and liberal, secular and religious, and Jewish and Arab.

This section goes one step deeper into Israel's multifaceted culture by making closer contact with Israel's diverse people, from Bedouin Arabs to Ethiopian Jews, from kibbutzniks to IDF soldiers, and from yeshiva scholars to Palestinian refugees. The story of Israel is also closely tied to its landmarks and ruins, such as the Dome of the Rock, Masada, Zippori, and the Western Wall.

Opposite: **In Galilee, an Arab family of olive-pickers takes a break in the shade.**

Below: **A group of Jewish schoolboys hangs out in the urban playground of Old Jerusalem.**

The Dead Sea

The Dead Sea, or Yam Hamelah (Sea of Salt), is the lowest place on Earth, averaging 1,312 feet (400 m) below sea level. Located on the deserted border between Israel and Jordan, the Dead Sea earned its name over two thousand years ago because its salty waters cannot support any animal or plant life; only bacteria can survive the Dead Sea's high salinity. Yet the Dead Sea has attracted human visitors for centuries, as a historical site associated with the ancient Israelite kingdom, the Roman Empire, and various biblical stories. Archaeologists believe that Sodom and Gomorrah, two cities destroyed by heaven for their wickedness (according to the Old Testament), may lie beneath the waters of the Dead Sea.

The source of the Dead Sea is actually the freshwater Jordan River, but millions of years of salt deposits and rapid evaporation have left behind a concentrated sea of salt. As Israeli and Jordanian farmers continue to divert water from the Jordan River for irrigation, the Dead Sea is shrinking at an alarming rate, and its waters are becoming even more mineral-rich. Israeli factories producing potash, magnesium, and calcium chloride have operated along the coast of the Dead Sea since 1929. In Kaliya,

Below: **The Dead Sea and its surroundings are mostly barren. Only plants that can tolerate scant rainfall and very salty soils grow on the banks of the Dead Sea.**

Left: **The Dead Sea Scrolls were first discovered by local shepherds in caves in the Judean Desert.**

where the Jordan River empties into the Dead Sea, tourist resorts advertise the supposed curative powers of the sea's water, mud, and sulfur springs.

Masada

Not far from the southwestern banks of the Dead Sea lie the ruins at Masada, a mountain fortress completed by Herod the Great, who ruled Judah from 37 B.C. to 4 B.C. In A.D. 70, the Romans sacked Jerusalem after revolts by Jewish zealots, who wished to overthrow their Roman rulers. The surviving zealots, outnumbered 15,000 to 1,000, held out at Masada for two more years before the Romans finally captured the fortress — only to find that the defenders had all committed suicide. Today, Masada is a popular tourist attraction and remains a symbol of Jewish pride.

The Dead Sea Scrolls

The Dead Sea Scrolls, discovered between 1947 and 1965 in the Judean Desert, are among the most important archaeological relics ever found. The contents of the scrolls, ranging from Hebrew manuscripts of the Old Testament to Greek legal documents, have allowed scholars to piece together Palestine's history between 250 B.C. and A.D. 70. Today, the Dead Sea Scrolls are kept in the Shrine of the Book at the Israel Museum in Jerusalem.

Below: **The scorching heat of the Jordan Valley causes a high rate of evaporation, which often results in beautiful formations of salt crystals in the Dead Sea.**

45

The Dome of the Rock

One of the most beautiful structures in Jerusalem, the Dome of the Rock is an Islamic monument that was built in the seventh century. It is the third holiest shrine in Islam, after the Ka'bah in Mecca and the Prophet's Mosque in Medina (both in Saudi Arabia). The Dome of the Rock is possibly the oldest Islamic building still standing.

The wooden dome of the shrine houses a large rock that plays a part in both Jewish and Islamic traditions. Jews believe Abraham (the patriarch of the Hebrews) prepared to sacrifice his son Isaac on the site of the rock. Muslims believe the Prophet Muhammad (the founder of Islam) rose to heaven from the rock. The Dome of the Rock stands on the original site of the Temple of Solomon, a Jewish shrine built in 957 B.C. In A.D. 70, the Romans destroyed the temple (which had already been rebuilt twice before), leaving behind the Western Wall as its sole remains. When Arab ruler Abd al-Malik finished building the Dome of the Rock in A.D. 691, he made the Western Wall part of a larger wall that surrounded the Dome of the Rock and al-Aqsa Mosque. The Western Wall has remained sacred to both Christians and Jews.

Opposite: **Muslims gather at the Dome of the Rock for prayers. Although it is a holy shrine for Muslims, the Dome of the Rock was not originally built as a mosque.**

Left: **The interior of the Dome of the Rock exhibits Moorish-influenced artwork. Between the seventh and eleventh centuries, Jerusalem was controlled by two different Muslim groups — the Arabs and the Moors, who were from North Africa.**

Israel Turns Fifty

In 1998, the State of Israel celebrated its fiftieth birthday with a grand display of fireworks, flag-waving, and performing arts. As Israeli air force jets streamed across the skies, patriotic drivers navigated the roads down below with Israeli flags fluttering from their cars. In Jerusalem, a national gala showcased the talents of the country's best dancers, musicians, writers, and artists. The performers used song and dance to reconstruct Israel's history — the Diaspora, the Zionist movement, the Holocaust, the post–World War II immigration, and the continuing efforts to achieve peace between Arabs and Israelis.

The birthday celebration extended well beyond Israel's national borders. Joint celebrations took place in France, Austria, Germany, and the United States and were linked together by television satellite. Israeli prime minister Benjamin Netanyahu delivered a keynote speech to a worldwide audience, thanking overseas supporters for standing by Israel during a half-century of war and peace.

Above: **Israelis celebrate their Independence Day with parades, songs, and dances.**

Israel Defense Forces (IDF)

Israel has fought five major wars since 1948 and remains as ready as ever to defend itself from foreign invaders. The IDF (made up of an air force, ground force, and navy) is headed by the Chief of the General Staff, who is responsible to the Minister of Defense.

Terms of Service

All Jewish and Druze men are required to serve for three years in the IDF once they reach the age of eighteen. Christians and Arabs serve on a volunteer basis. Military service is also compulsory for women, who are drafted for twenty-one months (also at the age of eighteen) but are barred from active combat duty; married women and women with children are exempt from IDF service.

Below: In May 1998, the IDF was called into East Jerusalem after outbreaks of Palestinian violence. Jerusalem and the Israeli-occupied territories (the Gaza Strip, the Golan Heights, and the West Bank) have a strong military presence to ensure the safety of civilians.

Left: **Unlike many other women in the world, Israeli women are required to serve in their national armed forces. Women make up a key component of the IDF.**

Israeli women remain on reserve duty until the age of twenty-four, while reserve duty for men lasts until the age of forty-nine. Reservists return to the army for a few weeks every year to maintain their military skills.

The reservists are the secret weapon of the IDF. Within a period of twenty-four hours, Israel can summon an army of several hundred thousand men and women. In previous attacks by Arab armies, the existing IDF soldiers were able to stand their ground before being strengthened by a massive wave of reinforcements. The IDF has never lost a major battle in the history of Israel.

Women in the IDF

Women have long been a part of Israel's military history. Before Israeli statehood, female Zionist soldiers guarded Jewish settlements and served in underground military organizations. During the 1948 war of independence, women fought side by side with men in the newly established IDF.

Today, female soldiers are no longer permitted on active combat missions, although many women in the IDF serve as combat instructors for new recruits. Other women soldiers fill valuable roles as technicians, intelligence specialists, computer operators, and doctors.

Jerusalem

The Holiest of Cities

One of the oldest cities in the world, Jerusalem is a spiritual and cultural center for Jews, Christians, and Muslims. For Jews, Jerusalem symbolizes the glory of both ancient Israel and the Zionist movement. For Christians, Jerusalem is the site of the crucifixion and resurrection of Jesus Christ. For Muslims, Jerusalem is the site of the sacred Dome of the Rock and is remembered as the first *qiblah* (KIB-lah), or direction in which Muslims face during prayers, before the Prophet Muhammad changed it to the Ka'bah (in Mecca) in A.D. 623.

Old Jerusalem is a tiny, but distinct, city within the city. Just 0.3 square miles (0.8 square km) in area, Old Jerusalem is the heart and soul of the capital, whose city limits now cover 42 square miles (109 square km). The Old City Wall, built by Suleiman the Magnificent of the Ottoman Empire, surrounds some of the oldest churches, temples, shrines, and fortresses ever built.

Below: **The Tower of David guards the western side of Old Jerusalem. The tower and the surrounding Citadel were built atop ruins dating back to the first century B.C., when Herod the Great ruled over Palestine.**

54

Left: **A traditional Jewish family walks along the busy streets of Jerusalem. Although Jerusalem has a very concentrated population of Hasidic Jews, non-Jewish residents make up almost 30 percent of the city's population.**

Old Jerusalem is divided into Christian, Jewish, Muslim, and Armenian quarters. Each of these districts is bustling with ethnic-flavored bazaars, or marketplaces, that contrast with the serenity of Old Jerusalem's many religious landmarks. The Mount of Olives, a famous Jewish burial ground and Christian pilgrimage site, overlooks Old Jerusalem from the east.

The Modern Israeli Capital

Jerusalem has come a long way since its first settlers arrived over five thousand years ago. Today, Jerusalem is Israel's political center (the seat of both the president and the Knesset) as well as a forum for scholars, bankers, and merchants. The Zionist immigration forced the city to expand in the late 1800s, resulting in a network of Russian, German, and American colonies just beyond the Old City Wall. Interspersed with these Jewish neighborhoods are Christian and Muslim communities of various ethnic backgrounds, making Jerusalem's population one of the most diverse in the world.

The Kibbutz

The kibbutz, or collective settlement, is a pillar of Israel's rural society. Founded in the early 1900s by immigrant Jews, the kibbutz movement was a bold experiment in lifestyle and economy. Today, kibbutzniks, or kibbutz residents, make up only 2.1 percent of the Israeli population, but their way of life is still the focus of much local and international interest.

The essence of the kibbutz is one big family that welcomes all types of people. For young couples, the kibbutz provides a socially secure environment for marrying and raising a family; working parents do not have to worry about job security, housing, or child care. For single young adults, the kibbutz offers a safe and democratic community, in which any hard-working person can help create a better society. For senior citizens, the

Left: **The kibbutz is not just an agricultural community. Many kibbutzim have diversified their economies to include small industries in textiles, furniture manufacturing, and even tourism.**

kibbutz is an active, close-knit neighborhood that welcomes the wisdom and leadership of its elders. Kibbutzniks live as a collective, sharing responsibilities, raising each other's children, and caring for each other in times of crisis. Money earned by the kibbutz is a group pocket that provides for all members' clothing, food, equipment, and material needs.

The Evolution of the Kibbutz

In the late 1800s, thousands of young Eastern European Jews began immigrating to Palestine. Some of these immigrants, inspired by the growing socialist movements in Poland and Russia, decided to create communities based on collectivist principles. They pooled their talents, incomes, resources, and labor in democratic, communal settlements.

The first kibbutz, Degania, was founded in 1909 near the shores of the Sea of Galilee. Several more kibbutzim were built

Below: **Young kibbutzniks enjoy a hayride during the festival of Shavuot, which celebrates the anniversary of when Moses received the Ten Commandments.**

at strategic locations and offered the first line of defense against Arab attacks. Many of Israel's political leaders, including current Prime Minister Ehud Barak, were raised on kibbutzim.

Currently, about 270 kibbutzim produce one-third of Israel's agricultural output, including fruits, vegetables, meats, and dairy products. More recently, some kibbutzim operate as guest houses, factories, or sites for cultural events. Kibbutzim are found mainly in Galilee, the Negev, and the Hills of Judea.

The Kings of Judah

David and Solomon, the greatest of the Israelite kings, ruled over Palestine almost three thousand years ago. Their reigns marked the golden age of ancient Israel — the unification of the Israelite tribes, the conquest of a Middle Eastern empire, and the installation of Jerusalem as the capital of Israel.

David

The son of a shepherd, David grew up in Bethlehem. He quickly made his name as a talented military leader, whose bravery in battle against the invading Philistines caught the attention of Saul, the first Israelite king and ruler of Judah (southern Palestine). David later married Saul's daughter, Michal, but his rising

Left: **The battle between David and Goliath is one of the most famous stories of the Bible. The young Israelite David killed Goliath, the Philistine giant, using just stones and a sling.**

Left: **Standing tall in the Negev, the Pillars of Solomon mark the site of a copper mine once used by King Solomon for commercial trade.**

popularity stirred the envy of his father-in-law, who tried to have him killed. David fled Judah, and, shortly after, Saul died on the battlefield after an ill-planned attack on the Philistine army.

David became the king of Judah in 1000 B.C. and soon conquered the neighboring Philistines, Edomites, Ammonites, and Jesubites (who had occupied Jerusalem). Over the course of his reign, which lasted thirty-nine years, he united the Israelites, founded a lasting dynasty, and became a respected leader in the history of civilization. King David's new capital, Jerusalem, would remain the spiritual and political center of the Israelites and their descendants, the Jews, throughout modern history.

Solomon

One of King David's many sons, Solomon succeeded his father to the throne in 961 B.C. Considered the most glorious of the Israelite kings, Solomon ruled Palestine for about thirty years. He was known as a legendary wise man, as well as an ambitious ruler with a taste for luxury. His most outstanding achievement was an extensive building program that transformed Jerusalem into a strongly fortified and stunningly beautiful city. Solomon shrewdly pursued commercial interests, strengthening his kingdom with trade alliances instead of relying just on military might. His famous mines contained not gold, but copper — a valuable trading commodity. Solomon was also a gifted writer, whose writings include the biblical books Proverbs and Ecclesiastes.

Below: **The Temple of Solomon, which once housed the Ark of the Covenant, was one of the most magnificent religious shrines ever built. Completed in 957 B.C., Solomon's temple (also known as the First Temple of Jerusalem) symbolized the vast wealth of the Israelite kingdom. Today, the Dome of the Rock, a Muslim shrine, stands on the old site of the Temple of Solomon.**

Minority Cultures

More than one-fifth of Israel's population is made up of non-Jews and Jews of non-European ancestry. These minorities represent a range of ethnic groups, religions, and lifestyles that contribute to Israel's unique national character.

Arabs

Numbering over 1.1 million people, Israel's Arab community is 75 percent Muslim, 16 percent Christian, and 9 percent Druze. Overall, Israeli Arabs maintain a separate existence from Israeli Jews through language (Arabic is Israel's second official language), a separate school system, Arabic mass media and literature, and an independent court system.

Left: **A Bedouin Arab makes himself a cup of tea.**

Muslim Arabs live mainly in the rural villages of northern Israel and the Negev. Some 70,000 of these Muslims are Bedouin Arabs, who traditionally wandered the deserts of Palestine and the Sinai Peninsula as cattle herders. The largest Christian Arab communities lie within northern cities, such as Nazareth and Haifa. The Druze, whose religion is closed to outsiders, maintain a close-knit social and religious community within Israel. The Druze settlements of Galilee are over eight hundred years old.

Circassians

Numbering about three thousand people, the Circassians are a Muslim group who remain separate from the Muslim Arab community. Originally from the Caucasus (a mountainous region north of Turkey and Iran), the Circassians fled their homeland after being conquered by the Russian Empire in 1864. Circassian communities also exist in Turkey, Syria, Jordan, and Iraq. Israeli Circassians are concentrated in Galilee and speak Arabic, Hebrew, and Kabardian (their native Circassian language).

Ethiopian Jews

Israel absorbed a total of 30,000 Ethiopian Jews (almost the entire Ethiopian Jewish community) in two major rescue missions — Operation Moses in 1984 and Operation Solomon in 1991. Along with Moroccan and Yemenite Jews, Ethiopian Jews demonstrate that Israel is a refuge for Jews of any race or color.

MINORITY SOLDIERS

Arabs are exempted from IDF service out of consideration for their family, religious, and cultural ties with the Arab world — Israel's primary threat. Volunteer military service among Arabs is encouraged, however, and some Arabs, notably the Bedouins, choose to participate. IDF service is mandatory for all Jewish and Druze men and women and all Circassian men.

Opera

Israel had an opera scene before it had independence — one of many examples of the tremendous artistic spirit of Jewish immigrants. The story of Israeli opera begins in Moscow, where Mordechai Golinkin composed *Vision of the Hebrew Art Temple of Opera in Palestine* in 1917. Six years later, Golinkin established the Palestine Opera, which debuted his masterpiece along with *La traviata* by Giuseppe Verdi. In 1945, U.S. soprano Edis de Philippe founded the Israel National Opera company (INO), which lasted until 1982 and helped launch the career of virtuoso Spanish tenor Placido Domingo.

The New Israeli Opera
The New Israeli Opera (NIO), founded in 1982 by the Ministry of Culture, has staged an impressive opera revival in the 1980s and 1990s. Installed in the Tel Aviv Performing Arts Center since 1994, the NIO rivals the Israel Philharmonic Orchestra as Israel's most prized cultural institution.

Below: **The New Israeli Opera is the leading opera company in Israel. The NIO stages contemporary Israeli operas as well as classical Italian operas.**

The NIO strives for artistic professionalism while also fostering a local Israeli talent pool. NIO productions often team up international opera stars with hometown Israeli artists — a combination that attracts enthusiasts of all ages and all levels of expertise. For Israeli opera artists, the NIO is a rewarding stepping stone to opera houses in foreign countries. For foreign opera artists, the NIO provides a beautiful theater hall, first-rate musicians and conductors, and a great opportunity for cultural exchange with Israeli audiences.

Above: **The Tel Aviv Performing Arts Center is home to Israel's national opera company, the New Israeli Opera (NIO).**

Immigrant Talent

Israel's influx of immigrants often includes gifted young musicians, singers, directors, dramatists, and set designers. Opera offers a challenging, dynamic, and appealing artistic outlet that requires a multidisciplinary ensemble. A number of famous Israeli opera singers, such as Gabi Sadeh, Marina Levitt, Mira Zakai, and Michal Shamir, launched their careers in the NIO. Former conductors include Shmuel Friedman, Yoav Talmi, Daniel Oren, and Asher Fish.

Palestinians

The inspiring story of how Israel was founded is accompanied by a tragic one — the plight of the Palestinians who have been displaced by the Jewish state. During the early 1900s, even as the Zionist immigration to Palestine steadily increased, the majority of the region's settlers were native Palestinian Arabs, who were unable to gain the international support that the Zionist Jews had earned. In 1946, Palestinian Arabs outnumbered immigrant Jews 1,270,000 to 680,000. Yet, in 1947, the United Nations recommended the partition of Palestine, with the Jews in control of the majority of the territory. In 1948, despite Palestinian objections, the Zionists established the State of Israel.

The 1948 war of independence left more than 700,000 Palestinians homeless and established a Jewish popular majority in Israel. Most of the Palestinian refugees settled in neighboring Jordan, Syria, Lebanon, and Egypt. Despite relief aid from the United Nations, the homeless Palestinians often suffered from

Below: **A Palestinian demonstrator in the Gaza Strip raises a portrait of Yasir Arafat, the chairman of the PLO.**

Left: An Israeli soldier pushes back a crowd of Palestinians in Jerusalem. Relations between Palestinians and Israelis have endured decades of embitterment and fear, which have led to many acts of violence.

poverty and discrimination in their host countries. In 1967, after the Six-Day War produced another 200,000 Palestinian refugees, the PLO, or Palestine Liberation Organization, was recognized as the Palestinians' official political body.

The PLO was formed to establish a democratic Palestinian state. In 1968, Yasir Arafat became the chairman of the PLO and began a terrorist campaign against Israel. After being forced out of Jordan by King Hussein in 1971, the PLO began operating out of Beirut, Lebanon, which became a command post for Palestinian terrorism. Despite the 1982 Israeli invasion of Lebanon, Arafat held on to the PLO leadership as he changed tactics, favoring diplomacy over terrorism as the means to achieve the PLO's goal.

On November 15, 1988, the PLO proclaimed the "State of Palestine," which, at the time, was a government that had no territorial base. In 1989, the PLO recognized Israel's right to exist and accepted the idea of independent Palestinian states (in the West Bank and the Gaza Strip) coexisting with Israel. Today, the PLO represents over 4 million Palestinians, whose dream of founding a Palestinian state is becoming a reality. The 1993 Israel-PLO accords, signed by Arafat and Israeli prime minister Yitzhak Rabin, were a breakthrough step in maintaining peace between Israeli Jews and Palestinians. In 1995, the Interim Israeli-Palestinian Agreement established the Palestinian Council, an elected, self-governing authority that oversees Palestinian affairs.

Below: Yasir Arafat, began his political career by cofounding Fatah, a leading PLO faction. After serving twenty years as the PLO's chairman, Arafat was elected president of the Palestinian state proclaimed in 1988. In 1994, after the signing of the Israel-PLO accords, Arafat shared the Nobel Prize for Peace with Israeli prime minister Yitzhak Rabin and foreign minister Shimon Peres.

Passover

Pesach, or Passover, is a celebration of Jewish history and religion that focuses on the Hebrews' deliverance from Egypt after years of slavery. The day before the Exodus, Egypt was struck by an evil plague that killed the firstborn members of each household. The Hebrew households, however, were protected by God, who let the plague pass over them — hence, the name *Passover*.

The purpose of Passover is for Jews to rejoice in their freedom and also feel the pain and suffering of their ancestors. During their hurried exodus from Egypt, the Hebrews had no time to wait for their bread to rise. This is why, during the seven days of Passover (for non-Israeli and Reform Jews, Passover lasts eight days), Jews are not allowed to eat leavened bread, or bread that has been allowed to rise. Instead, they eat matzo, a kind of flat, unleavened bread.

Left: **Moses** *(top panel, center)* **was the prophet who led the Hebrews out of Egypt and then delivered the Ten Commandments to them at Mount Sinai. The commandments were engraved on two stone tablets that were later housed in the Ark of the Covenant** *(bottom panel, right).*

Left: **A rabbi inspects matzo, or unleavened bread, for Passover. Matzo is baked in the form of large, thin crackers.**

The Seder

The *seder* (SAY-der), which means "order" in Hebrew, is a ceremonial family meal held on the first night of Passover. (Non-Israeli Jews hold another seder on the second night of Passover.) The head of the family leads the seder service, which is a narration and reenactment of the Hebrews' Exodus from Egypt. After the family recites a benediction, or *Kiddush* (KEY-dush), the youngest child of the family asks four questions about Passover that are answered in unison by the entire family. The reciting of these answers tells the story of the Hebrews' plight. This story, known as the Haggadah, is repeated every year during the seder. The Haggadah is followed by the eating of matzo and bitter herbs, or *maror* (MAH-rohr), which are dipped in a mixture of crushed fruits and wine. This symbolic ritual allows the participants to experience the bitterness and sacrifice of the Hebrews, who were eventually rewarded by God for their perseverance.

Finally, the family takes part in the hearty seder dinner, which includes gefilte fish, sweet potatoes, beef, and *tzimmes* (TSIM-iss) — a casserole made of vegetables and fruits. The meal is followed by prayers, psalm readings, folk songs, and wine-drinking, each of which expresses thanks to God for the Hebrews' liberation and the survival of the Jewish people.

Talmudic Studies

The Talmud

The Talmud is a collection of academic writings on Jewish law and morality. More than 1,500 years ago, Jewish scholars in Babylonia and Palestine compiled their interpretations of the Mishna, an oral code of laws that had been passed down through generations of the Jewish community until A.D. 200, when it was written down. The Palestinian scholars produced the first Talmud, while their Babylonian counterparts, whose Talmud is longer and more detailed, finished a hundred years later. Collectively, the Talmud represents one of the most studied works of Judaic literature.

Yeshivas

The first officially named yeshiva, or religious academy for Jewish boys and men, was founded in Jerusalem in the first century A.D. This began a long and prestigious history of Jewish

Below: **Yeshiva scholars gather at a synagogue in Jerusalem.**

scholarship that later spread to Europe, the Middle East, and North America. Today, yeshivas remain important in shaping and defining the boundaries of Jewish religious life. The world's leading yeshivas are located in Israel and the United States.

Talmudic studies at yeshivas involve extensive discussion and analysis of the Torah, the Talmud, and various works of religious commentary and criticism; in addition, students are required to study a separate, secular academic curriculum. From age four until several years after they marry (and sometimes throughout their adult lives), most Yeshiva scholars spend long hours each day reading, learning, and debating holy texts. The Jewish community places a high value on religious scholars and teachers. With the help of generous government grants, student enrollment in Israeli yeshivas has grown to over 50,000.

Left: **Young boys in a yeshiva kindergarten class enjoy their precious playtime.**

The Western Wall

The Western Wall, also known as the Wailing Wall, is one of the most sacred sites in Jerusalem, along with the Dome of the Rock and the Holy Sepulcher (the site of Christ's crucifixion and burial tomb). Measuring 160 feet (49 m) in length and 60 feet (18 m) in height, the Western Wall is all that remains of the Second Temple of Jerusalem, which had been built by the Jews to replace the First Temple of Jerusalem, built by King Solomon. This historical and symbolic link to the ancient Israelite kingdom makes the Western Wall the holiest place in Judaism.

From Solomon to the Six-Day War

King Solomon constructed the First Temple of Jerusalem in 957 B.C. In 586 B.C., it was looted and destroyed by the Babylonians, who then exiled the Israelites to Babylonia. After Cyrus the Great of Persia conquered Babylonia in 539 B.C., he permitted the Jews to return to their homeland and rebuild the temple. The Second Temple of Jerusalem, finished in 515 B.C., was desecrated by the Romans in 54 B.C. The rebuilding of the Second Temple, begun by Herod the Great, lasted until A.D. 26. In A.D. 70, after crushing a rebellion by the Jewish zealots, the Romans destroyed the Second Temple, which would never again be rebuilt.

The Western Wall is a section of the rampart that once surrounded Herod's rebuilt temple and has attracted Jewish pilgrims since the fall of the Roman Empire in A.D. 476. Controlled by Jordan from 1948 to 1967, the Western Wall was captured by Israeli paratroopers in the Six-Day War of 1967.

Holy Ground in a Land of Conflict

Today, the Western Wall remains a sacred pilgrimage site for all Jews. Anyone can touch the stones of the wall, but women must pray separately from men. A traditional custom among Jews is to place a small piece of paper containing one's prayers between the crevices of the wall's blocks. Although Jews regard the Western Wall as holy ground, it lies in East Jerusalem (formerly occupied by Jordan and now occupied by Israel), a territory that has seen its share of violence between Arabs and Jews. Guns and prayer books are often stacked side by side near the wall, while Jewish soldiers and civilians say their prayers.

Above: **A Jew spends a moment in prayer by the Western Wall. After observing the emotional and, often, mournful prayers of devoted Jews at the Western Wall, foreigners began referring to it as the Wailing Wall.**

Opposite: **Jews gather at the Western Wall for prayers. Originally, the Western Wall was part of a longer wall that protected the Second Temple of Jerusalem. Today, the Western Wall makes up a section of the outer wall surrounding the Dome of the Rock and the Al-Aqsa Mosque.**

Zippori

The Jewel of Galilee

Zippori, also known by its Greek name, Sepphoris, is the ancient capital of Galilee and an archaeological window into the past. The ruins of Zippori are located on a hill in Lower Galilee, about 3 miles (5 km) west of Nazareth. Unlike Jerusalem and Masada, which were destroyed by the armies of the Roman Empire, Zippori was spared by the Romans.

Between the first and seventh centuries A.D., Zippori thrived as a center for Jewish culture and education. Talmudic literature describes Zippori as a beautiful and sophisticated city, home to scholars, sages, artists, and writers. In A.D. 363, Zippori was destroyed by an earthquake, but it was quickly rebuilt by the

Left: **The ruins at Zippori are just one of more than 3,500 registered archaeological sites within Israel.**

Left: **A team of archaeologists measures the dimensions of a mosaic discovered in Zippori.**

Jews and later survived the fall of the Roman Empire in A.D. 456. After the Arabs invaded Palestine in the seventh century, however, Zippori fell into ruin and disrepair.

Reconstructing the Past

By studying the ruins of Zippori, archaeologists are trying to visualize what life was like in ancient Palestine. Recent excavations have revealed a synagogue, a basilica, a theater, churches, bath houses, and a number of private villas. Zippori is most famous for its beautiful mosaics, some of which paved the streets and sidewalks of the city. Over forty mosaics, each more than 1,500 years old, have been discovered so far.

An International Learning Experience

The Israeli National Parks Authority opened Zippori to the public in 1992. Today, the site continues to attract tourists and scholars from all over the world. The Institute of Archaeology at Hebrew University of Jerusalem currently heads a research expedition at Zippori and offers a variety of courses featuring field work and workshops at the actual excavation site. The Sepphoris Regional Project, sponsored by Duke University, Wake Forest University, and the University of Connecticut, allows U.S. archaeology students to get a hands-on learning experience with the treasures of Zippori.

RELATIONS WITH NORTH AMERICA

Israel has always had close ties with North America — especially the United States, which, like Israel, has a strong commitment to democracy, a melting-pot immigrant culture, and a tradition of outstanding political leadership. Since the late 1960s, the United States has faithfully stood by Israel's side. U.S. government officials have defended Israel's right to exist, joined Israel in its fight against terrorism, and served as mediators for Arab-Israeli peace negotiations. Israel currently receives U.S. $3 billion in annual military and economic aid from the U.S. government, and joint ventures between Israeli and U.S. industries have grown steadily since the 1985 Israel-United States Free Trade Agreement. U.S.-Israeli relations also include various cultural exchanges among scholastic, religious, artistic, and athletic groups.

Like the United States, Canada quickly recognized the State of Israel after its independence and, today, enjoys healthy trade relations with Israel. Overall, Israeli-American relations are bolstered by a large and supportive Jewish community in both the United States and Canada. Many Jewish-Americans maintain familial, business, or cultural links with Israel.

Opposite: **A Jewish bakery in Manhattan sells fresh knishes and bagels. New York City's most famous Jewish neighborhoods are Brighton Beach (an enclave of Russian immigrant Jews) and Borough Park (home of the United States' largest community of Hasidic Jews).**

Left: **In July 1994, U.S. president Bill Clinton** *(center)* **met with Jordan's King Hussein** *(left)* **and Israeli prime minister Yitzhak Rabin** *(right)* **to negotiate the Jordan-Israel peace treaty. This ended a forty-six-year state of war between the two countries. U.S. politicians and diplomats have been instrumental in assisting the peace process between Arabs and Israelis.**

Early U.S.-Israeli Relations

Immediately after Israel declared its independence in 1948, U.S. president Harry S. Truman officially recognized the new nation and established friendly U.S.-Israeli relations. As Arab-Israeli conflicts escalated, however, the United States joined other Western nations in an arms embargo against all Middle Eastern countries — an attempt to reduce the military and political tension in the region.

The 1948 war of independence was a huge setback for the Israeli economy, which had to provide for a rapidly growing immigrant population. Despite the arms embargo, Israel received financial aid from many American sources, including the U.S. government, commercial banks, and diaspora Jews. With these generous loans and donations, the Israeli government built housing settlements, city infrastructures, a shipping fleet, and a national airline. Between 1948 and 1952, Israel's Jewish population grew from 650,000 to 1.4 million.

Above: U.S. president Harry S. Truman, who was in office from 1945 to 1953, supported the new State of Israel with financial aid and diplomatic recognition.

Left: An elderly Israeli settler sits beside a tree he has planted in the Negev. American funding helped support the afforestation of Israel's barren lands.

Partners in Arms

Through the 1960s and early 1970s, Israel endured wars, terrorist acts, and continual threats to national security. In 1965, President Lyndon B. Johnson lifted the U.S. arms embargo against Israel and shifted U.S. diplomatic policy toward strengthening Israel with military firepower, and not just monetary aid. Armed with U.S. weapons, the IDF won the Six-Day War of 1967 and the Yom Kippur War of 1973, both of which secured new territorial gains for Israel. Following the Yom Kippur War, the United States assisted Israel, Egypt, and Syria in the disengagement agreements, which stationed U.N. forces along the respective border zones.

Despite continuing armed clashes between the Arabs and Israelis, the U.S. government maintained its policy of supplying arms to Israel, reasoning that a strong Israel was essential to achieving peace in the Middle East. Toward the late 1970s, the United States assumed a more active role in brokering peace between Israel and its Arab neighbors.

Below: **IDF soldiers used U.S. military equipment, such as these Sherman tanks, to defend Israeli territory during the Yom Kippur War.**

The Camp David Accords

In November 1977, Egyptian president Anwar Sadat made a historic visit to Jerusalem, where he revealed to the Knesset his intentions to reach a peace settlement with Israel. Israeli prime minister Menachem Begin agreed to collaborate with Sadat, whose strategy was opposed by most of his Arab allies.

In September 1978, Begin and Sadat met with U.S. president Jimmy Carter at Camp David, Maryland, to work out a framework for peaceful relations between Israel and Egypt. The resulting Camp David Accords were a landmark in Arab-Israeli relations and set the stage for the Egypt-Israel Peace Treaty, which was signed by both countries in Washington, D.C., on March 26, 1979. Israel received full diplomatic recognition from Egypt but was required to withdraw from the territories it had seized in the Six-Day War and eventually grant self-rule to the Palestinians living in the West Bank and the Gaza Strip. Meanwhile, Egypt regained its lost territories but was allowed only a limited military presence in these areas. For their heroic efforts, Sadat and Begin received the Nobel Prize for Peace in 1978.

Below: **On March 26, 1979, Egyptian president Anwar Sadat** *(left)*, **U.S. president Jimmy Carter** *(center)*, **and Israeli prime minister Menachem Begin** *(right)* **signed the historic peace treaty that had been negotiated at Camp David, Maryland.**

Despite the assassination of President Sadat on October 6, 1971, Egypt fulfilled its terms of the peace agreement and assumed full control of the Sinai Peninsula by April 1982. Unfortunately, Sadat's bold step toward peace did not represent an entire change in Arab attitudes toward Israel. In response to repeated attacks by PLO terrorists, the IDF invaded Lebanon in 1982, occupying it until 1985. Yet the peace process tentatively continued in the mid-1980s, as the United States mediated talks between Israel and a joint Palestinian-Jordanian delegation. The success of the Camp David Accords, however, remained elusive in handling these negotiations.

Above: **Ramat Gan, in eastern Israel, was hit by Iraqi missiles during the Persian Gulf War of 1991. The Israelis did not counterattack — a choice that prevented the war from erupting into a new Arab-Israeli clash. After destroying the Iraqi defenses, U.S. president George Bush declared a cease-fire on February 28, 1991.**

The Persian Gulf War

On August 2, 1990, Iraqi armies invaded Kuwait, thus postponing the prospects for peace in the Middle East. The Persian Gulf War began on January 16, 1991, as the United States initiated Operation Desert Storm, an aerial bombing campaign against Iraqi air defenses. The Israeli government supported the U.S. war effort but did not take part in the military operations, even after Iraq began targeting missile attacks at Israel.

Expanding the U.S. Peacekeeping Role

In October 1991, the United States and the Soviet Union sponsored the Madrid Peace Conference, which fielded Israeli, Lebanese, Syrian, Jordanian, and Palestinian representatives. This ambitious meeting set the wheels spinning for successive Arab-Israeli peace talks hosted by the United States.

The administration of President Bill Clinton has played an important role in the Middle East peace process by supporting the Israel-PLO accords of 1993, the Jordan-Israel peace treaty of 1994, and the Syrian-Israeli negotiations of 1995 and 1996. In the Israel-PLO accords, signed by PLO chairman Yasir Arafat and Israeli prime minister Yitzhak Rabin in Washington, D.C., the PLO renounced the use of terrorism and acknowledged Israel's right to exist, while Israel recognized the PLO as the sole representative of the Palestinian people. Both sides agreed to a set of guidelines for a five-year interim period of Palestinian self-government.

After Rabin's assassination in 1995, the Israeli government, led by Prime Minister Benjamin Netanyahu, took a more conservative stance on Israeli-Palestinian negotiations. As the Arabs and Israelis continue their search for common ground, the United States remains committed to achieving peace in the region.

Left: **On December 5, 1994, General John Shalikashvili** *(right)*, **chairman of the U.S. military Joint Chiefs of Staff, met with Ehud Barak** *(left)*, **then Israeli Chief of the General Staff, in Tel Aviv to discuss security measures that would ensure peace between Israel and Syria. Barak was elected prime minister of Israel in May 1999.**

Canada and Israel

In international politics, Canada often expresses support for Israel through its pro-Israel stance in various United Nations forums. Friendly Canadian-Israeli relations have been enhanced by a range of joint scientific ventures and cultural exchanges. The Israeli Ministry of Foreign Affairs regularly promotes Israeli cultural activities in Canada, such as art exhibitions, theatrical performances, music concerts, and Hebrew classes.

Trade and Industrial Relations

Israel exports 46 percent of its goods and services to Europe and over 30 percent to North America. In total, Israel's export trade is worth U.S. $31.3 billion. Ties between U.S. and Israeli industrial firms have been fostered by the U.S.-Israeli Binational Science Foundation (BSF) and the U.S.-Israel Binational Industrial Research and Development Foundation (BIRD-F), which offer funding for joint research projects ranging from computer graphics to biomedical engineering.

Above: **An Israeli teacher instructs her computer-literate students. Technology has been the key to Israel's current trade ties.**

Below: **Israeli prime minister Yitzhak Rabin *(left)* met with Canadian prime minister Jean Chrétien *(right)* in 1993.**

The World Jewish Community

Although the State of Israel was founded as the Jewish homeland, most of the world's Jews reside elsewhere and are often well-integrated into foreign cultures. The world Jewish population stands at approximately 13 million, with 34 percent living in Israel, 50 percent in North and South America, and 15 percent in Europe. During the 1980s and 1990s, Israel absorbed over 700,000 immigrants, mostly from the former Soviet Union, Eastern Europe, and Ethiopia. Jewish-Americans make up just a small fraction of the vast numbers of Jews immigrating to Israel.

Totaling over 5 million people, the U.S. Jewish community is the largest in the world and has been instrumental in supporting Israeli interests (both independently and through the U.S. government). The United Jewish Appeal (UJA), based in the United States, is one of the main fund-raising agencies for the World Zionist Organization (WZO), which was founded at the first Zionist Congress, held in Switzerland in 1897. Today, the WZO serves as a valuable liaison to the Jewish diaspora by facilitating immigration, promoting Jewish education and culture worldwide, and defending the rights of all Jews.

Below: **At the fifth Maccabiah Games, or Jewish Olympics, held in 1957, over twenty national teams arrived in Tel Aviv to compete. Athletics provide a spirited and entertaining avenue for cross-cultural exchange between Jews from all over the world.**

Left: **Tourists go for a dusty camel ride in the Negev. Other favorite tourist destinations include Jerusalem, the Sea of Galilee, Eilat, and the Dead Sea.**

Tourism and Cultural Exchange

North Americans make up 23 percent of the 2.1 million tourists who visit Israel every year. One of the fastest growing industries in Israel, tourism earns U.S. $2.8 billion annually and brings in a diverse group of people with interests in history, religion, politics, archaeology, and wildlife.

Israel also hosts a variety of professional conferences that attract foreign businessmen, scientists, writers, and teachers. Israel's international cultural ties are manifested in cultural agreements with over 70 countries. Athletic tournaments, student and academic exchanges, film festivals, art workshops, and book fairs are just a few of Israel's many cultural exchange programs.

Itzhak Perlman

One of the most famous Israeli-Americans today is virtuoso violinist Itzhak Perlman, who was born in Tel Aviv in 1945. Perlman received his first violin lessons at the Tel Aviv Academy of Music. A gifted prodigy, he staged his first public concert in Israel at the age of ten, and, in 1958, he began his studies at the Juilliard School of Music in New York City. He made his Carnegie Hall debut in 1963, and, a year later, he began an extensive national tour, performing with major American orchestras. In January 1965, he returned to Israel for a series of concerts with the Israel Philharmonic Orchestra.

Over the next three decades, Perlman remained based in New York City and continued to perform and record vigorously. He recorded chamber music with fellow world-class musicians, such as U.S. violinist Isaac Stern, U.S. cellist Yo-Yo Ma, Israeli pianist Daniel Barenboim, and Russian pianist Vladimir Ashkenazy. Perlman also experimented with nonclassical musical forms, such as jazz and ragtime. In the meantime, his frequent appearances at benefit concerts, awards ceremonies, and talk shows made him a household name to Americans.

Above: **One of the greatest violinists in the world, Itzhak Perlman is known for his brilliant technique and his passionate concerts.**

In 1986, Perlman received the U.S. Medal of Freedom — the highest decoration that can be awarded to a civilian — for his outstanding artistic achievement. Perlman has fostered Israeli-American cultural relations through his enduring support of the Israel Philharmonic Orchestra.

Pinchas Zukerman

A close friend of Itzhak Perlman, Israeli-American musician Pinchas Zukerman has earned an impressive reputation as a virtuoso violinist, violist, and conductor. Born in 1948 in Tel Aviv, Zukerman began learning the violin at the age of seven. After attending the Israel Conservatory of Music and the Tel Aviv Academy of Music, Zukerman studied at the Juilliard School between 1962 and 1967. He toured North America and Europe as a soloist and then began his conducting career, working with the English Chamber Orchestra, the St. Paul Chamber Orchestra, and a number of symphony orchestras in America and Europe. Today, Zukerman is the artistic director of the Pinchas Zukerman Performance Program at the Manhattan School of Music.

Below: **Violinist Pinchas Zukerman *(left)* embraces Indian-American conductor Zubin Mehta *(right)* after playing at the 1982 Huberman Festival, which celebrated the one-hundredth anniversary of the birth of Israel Philharmonic Orchestra founder, Bronislaw Huberman.**

ISREL

LEBANON

SYRIA

▲ Mount Hermon
(9,232 ft/2,814 m)

GOLAN
HEIGHTS

Mount Meron
(3,964 ft/1,208 m) ▲ Zefat

GALILEE

Acre ● ● Karmiel

Haifa ● ∴ Zippori
● Nazareth

*Sea of
Galilee*

Mount Carmel
(1,791 ft/546 m) ▲

● Degania

Caesarea ∴

MEDITERRANEAN

Netanya ●

SEA

SAMARIA

Ramat Gan ●
Tel Aviv-Yafo ●
Bat Yam ● ● Holon

WEST
BANK

Mount of Olives
(2,652 ft/808 m) ▲

Jordan

Jordan Valley

Rehovot ●

Ashdod ● ■ JERUSALEM
● Bethlehem

● Jericho
● Kaliya

Judean Desert

*Dead
Sea*

GAZA
STRIP

● Gaza

● Hebron

Hills of Judea

● En Gedi
∴ Masada

JUDEA

● Beersheba

N E G E V

Arava Valley

EGYPT

JORDAN

S I N A I   P E N I N S U L A

State Boundary	
Provincial Boundary	
Equator	
■ Capital	
● City	
∴ Historical Site	
River	

N

● Eilat

Gulf of Aqaba

Above: Haifa, in northwestern Israel, has many beautiful beaches along the Mediterranean Sea.

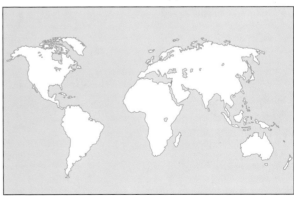

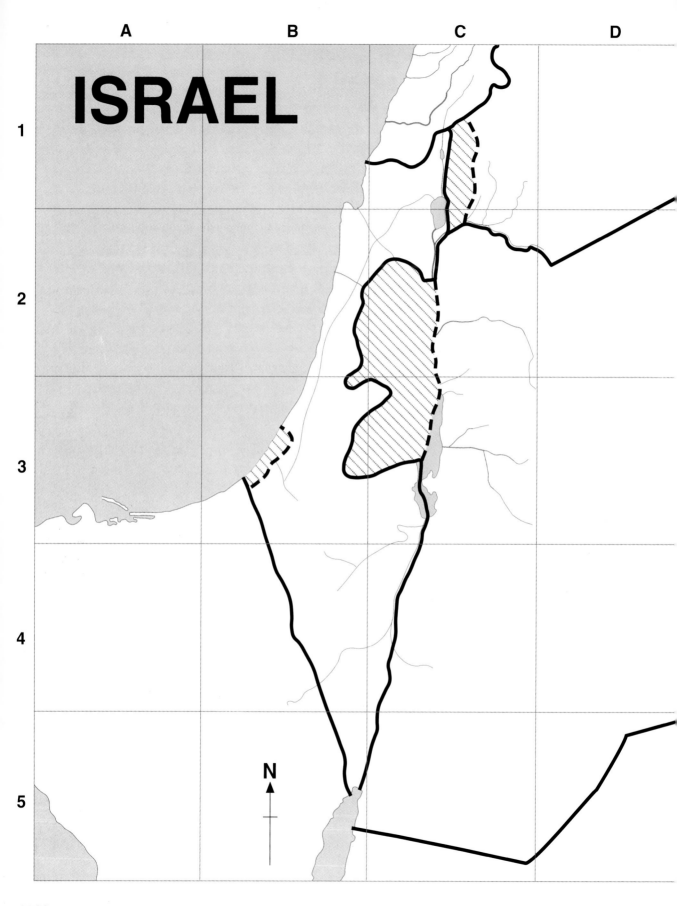

ISRAEL

A B C D

1
2
3
4
5

N

How Is Your Geography?

Learning to identify the main geographical areas and points of a country can be challenging. Although it may seem difficult at first to memorize the locations and spellings of major cities or the names of mountain ranges, rivers, deserts, lakes, and other prominent physical features, the end result of this effort can be very rewarding. Places you previously did not know existed will suddenly come to life when referred to in world news, whether in newspapers, television reports, or other books and reference sources. This knowledge will make you feel a bit closer to the rest of the world, with its fascinating variety of cultures and physical geography.

Used in a classroom setting, the instructor can make duplicates of this map using a copy machine. (PLEASE DO NOT WRITE IN THIS BOOK!) Students can then fill in any requested information on their individual map copies. Used one-on-one, the student can also make copies of the map on a copy machine and use them as a study tool. The student can practice identifying place names and geographical features on his or her own.

Below: **The city of Nazareth is a center for Arab traders and Christian pilgrims.**

Israel at a Glance

Official Name   Medinat Yisra'el, State of Israel

Capital   Jerusalem

Official Languages   Hebrew, Arabic

Population   5.8 million (1998 estimate)

Land Area   7,992 square miles (20,699 square kilometers)

Highest Point   Mount Meron 3,964 feet (1,208 meters)

Major River   Jordan

Lakes and Seas   Dead Sea, Sea of Galilee (Lake Kinneret)

Major Cities   Bat Yam, Beersheba, Haifa, Holon, Jerusalem, Tel Aviv-Yafo

Head of Government   The prime minister (Ehud Barak as of 1999)

Famous Leaders   David (d. 962 B.C.), Solomon (mid-tenth century B.C.),
          Herod the Great (73 B.C.–4 B.C.), Theodor Herzl (1860–1904),
          David Ben-Gurion (1886–1973), Golda Meir (1898–1978),
          Menachem Begin (1913–1992), Yitzhak Rabin (1922–1995),
          Shimon Peres (1923–), Benjamin Netanyahu (1949–)

Major Religions   Bahaism, Christianity (Greek Catholic, Greek Orthodox,
          Roman Catholic), Druze, Islam (Sunni), Judaism
          (Conservative, Orthodox, Reform)

Holy Sites   Dome of the Rock, Church of the Holy Sepulcher,
          Mount of Olives, Mount Tabor, Western Wall

Religious Holidays   Christmas, Easter, Good Friday (Christian); Hanukkah,
          Passover, Purim, Rosh Hashanah, Sukkot, Yom Kippur,
          (Jewish); Eid al-Adha, Eid al-Fitr, Ramadan (Muslim)

Secular Holidays   Holocaust Memorial Day, Independence Day, Memorial Day

Major Industries   Chemicals, computer software, diamond polishing, electronics,
          telecommunications, textiles

Currency   New Israeli shekel (4.03 NIS = U.S. $1 as of 1999)

Opposite: **The St. George Monastery, located near Jerusalem, was built in the sixth century.**